Dirty Jobs
Mechanic

Simon Rose

MEDIA ENHANCED BOOKS
AV2 BY WEIGL™
ADDED VALUE • AUDIO VISUAL

www.av2books.com

AV² provides enriched content that supplements and complements this book. Weigl's AV² books strive to create inspired learning and engage young minds in a total learning experience.

Your AV² Media Enhanced books come alive with...

Audio
Listen to sections of the book read aloud.

Key Words
Study vocabulary, and complete a matching word activity.

Video
Watch informative video clips.

Quizzes
Test your knowledge.

Go to **www.av2books.com**, and enter this book's unique code.

Embedded Weblinks
Gain additional information for research.

Slide Show
View images and captions, and prepare a presentation.

BOOK CODE

Z893795

AV² by Weigl brings you media enhanced books that support active learning.

Try This!
Complete activities and hands-on experiments.

... and much, much more!

Published by AV² by Weigl
350 5th Avenue, 59th Floor
New York, NY 10118

Websites: www.av2books.com www.weigl.com

Library of Congress Cataloging-in-Publication Data

Rose, Simon, 1961-
 Mechanic / Simon Rose.
   pages cm. -- (Dirty jobs)
 Includes bibliographical references and index.
 ISBN 978-1-4896-2990-6 (hard cover : alk. paper) -- ISBN 978-1-4896-2991-3 (soft cover : alk. paper) -- ISBN 978-1-4896-2992-0 (single user ebook) -- ISBN 978-1-4896-2993-7 (multi-user ebook)
 1. Automobiles--Maintenance and repair--Juvenile literature. 2. Automobiles--Maintenance and repair--Vocational guidance--Juvenile literature. 3. Automobile mechanics--Juvenile literature. I. Title.
 TL152.R655 2016
 629.28'7023--dc23
                        2014038986

Printed in the United States of America in Brainerd, Minnesota
1 2 3 4 5 6 7 8 9 0 19 18 17 16 15

012015
WEP051214

Senior Editor: Aaron Carr
Designer: Mandy Christiansen

Every reasonable effort has been made to trace ownership and to obtain permission to reprint copyright material. The publishers would be pleased to have any errors or omissions brought to their attention so that they may be corrected in subsequent printings.

Weigl acknowledges Getty Images as its primary image supplier for this title.

Contents

What Is a Mechanic?

Mechanics inspect, repair, and maintain all types of vehicles. They mostly work with cars, vans, and trucks. Mechanics are also known as auto mechanics or service technicians.

Mechanics repair or replace vehicle parts when they are broken. They also do maintenance checks. These checks make sure a vehicle is working properly. It is important to have these checks done regularly. This helps stop problems before they happen.

Mechanics need to know all about different **makes** of vehicles. They might work with different parts of a vehicle. These include engines, electrical systems, computer systems, or **bodywork**. A mechanic can be an expert in all or just some of these areas. Although most vehicles run on **gasoline** or **diesel**, mechanics might also work on vehicles that run on **ethanol** or electricity.

There were 701,100 mechanics in the United States in 2012.

Mechanics have to pass Automotive Service Excellence (ASE) tests to work in many places.

About 14 percent of mechanics work for themselves.

Some mechanics are experts in certain makes of vehicle. They work closely with the vehicle manufacturer.

Where They Work

Most mechanics work in auto repair shops. Some work for small repair companies. Others work for car **dealerships** that sell new and used cars. Mechanics also work for companies that have vehicle **fleets**. These companies have their own repair and maintenance shops. Some are private companies, and some are owned by the government.

About 70 percent of auto mechanics work in shops, dealerships, or in parts stores.

Most mechanics work full-time. Working **overtime** outside the normal working week is also common.

Repair shops often have large doors that open up the garage to the outside. This brings in light and fresh air. Mechanics need plenty of light to see under cars and vehicle hoods. They also need to keep engine fumes from building up inside.

Some mechanics work on aircraft or military vehicles.

A Dirty Job

Mechanics work with greasy parts and tools. They sometimes have to crawl under cars or reach down into dirty engines. Mechanics are often covered in dirt and grease by the end of the day.

Auto repair shops can also be dangerous. Mechanics can get small cuts, sprains, and bruises. They can be hurt by **power tools**. They might also be burned by **welding** equipment. Mechanics work with dangerous chemicals or fumes. These come from brake fluids, **lubricants**, and paint. Mechanics might breathe in **exhaust** fumes or dust from lead or **asbestos**. These can cause serious health problems.

Machines called lifts raise cars into the air. This makes it easier for mechanics to see what they are working on.

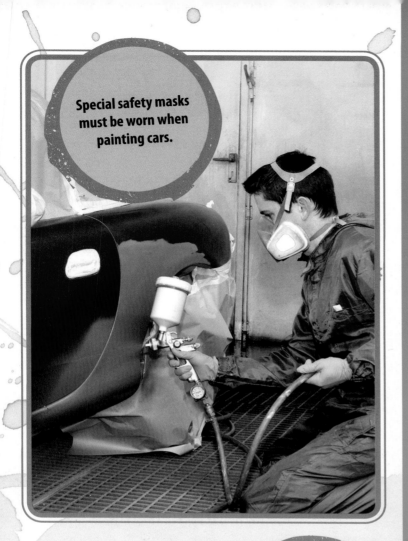

Special safety masks must be worn when painting cars.

Before starting a job, mechanics work out how much the job will cost. This is called an estimate.

Accidents and Injuries

A mechanic's workplace can be hazardous. Mechanics can sometimes be hurt by the equipment they use.

Mechanics are more likely to be **injured** at work than most other workers in the United States. The most common injuries are **cuts**, **sprains**, and **bruises**.

About **900,000** U.S. auto mechanics have had to work with asbestos dust.

Employers must give workers **hearing protection** if they are to work for **two hours** or more with **loud noise**. Sometimes, the noise can be as loud as a **lawnmower**.

All in a Day's Work

Mechanics might do repair, servicing, or maintenance work on an average day. The mechanic asks the owner about the vehicle's problem. The mechanic also learns about the problem from sounds or smells. They might take the vehicle for a test drive to learn more. The mechanic then looks for the cause of the problem. Computer equipment can be used to test parts and systems. This is to make sure that they are working properly. Some parts of the vehicle might need to be taken apart. These parts include tires, brakes, steering, exhaust, or **suspension** parts. Mechanics might need to replace electrical wiring, belts, and hoses. Some mechanics repair or paint vehicle bodywork.

Mechanics also check repairs that have been done before. The mechanic might check tire pressure and change the oil and **filters**. This work helps prevent problems before they occur. When all the work is done, the mechanic explains everything to the owner of the vehicle.

Before they begin, mechanics tell the owner of the vehicle about the work that will be done.

A tune-up is carried out on an engine to improve performance.

A 2014 survey for National Car Care Month found that 79% of cars needed some kind of service or repair.

The three things that are most often in need of servicing are oil changes, air filter replacements, and brake repairs.

The Auto Repair Process

The steps a mechanic takes to fix a vehicle may change from job to job. Some problems can be fixed in one day. Other problems may take several days or even weeks to fix.

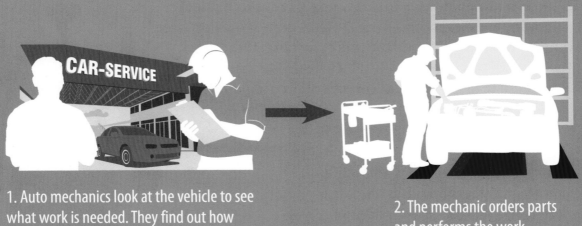

1. Auto mechanics look at the vehicle to see what work is needed. They find out how much the work will cost. After the owner agrees, work can start.

2. The mechanic orders parts and performs the work.

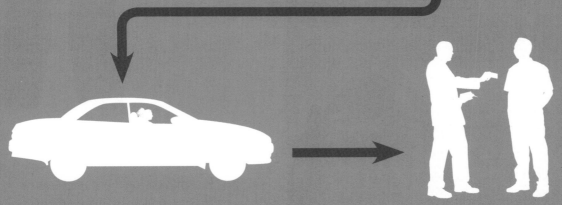

3. Some of these are done in the repair shop. Others are done on the road during test drives. More work is done if needed.

4. The customer collects the car and makes a payment for the work.

Staying Safe

Tools and hazards in the workplace can injure mechanics. They wear safety equipment to protect their skin, eyes, ears, and lungs. Many companies provide equipment and uniforms for their workers. Others ask mechanics to buy their own safety gear. Mechanics also have safety training and follow safety procedures.

Coveralls

Coveralls are one-piece outfits worn over a mechanic's clothes. Coveralls are made from long-lasting material. Some are fireproof. Coveralls protect against dirt, splashes, and spills. Coveralls have pockets for tools. Many have side vents. These allow access to the mechanic's pockets underneath the coveralls.

Facemasks

Facemasks stop mechanics from breathing in dust and dangerous fumes from chemicals. Some facemasks filter air. Others are supplied with fresh air. Some are only used once. Others can be reused.

Gloves

Mechanics wear fabric or leather gloves when welding metal. They also use these when working with hot exhaust pipes. Rubber gloves are used when mechanics need to feel parts of the vehicle with their fingertips. They also stop oils and chemicals from going into the skin. Rubber gloves can be thrown away.

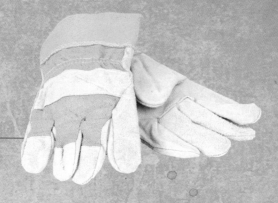

Eye Protection

Mechanics can have eye injuries from chemicals or from flying pieces of metal. Safety glasses or goggles protect their eyes. Face shields are also used. These protect the face and neck. Repair shops usually have an eyewash station. Mechanics can clean their eyes with water in an emergency.

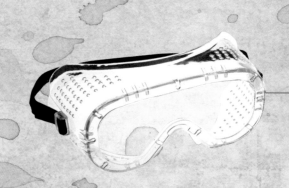

Ear Protection

Auto repair shops can be very noisy. Mechanics wear earplugs that fit inside the ears. For better protection they use headphones. These fit over the outside of the ears. Headphones block out more noise than small earplugs.

Tools of the Trade

Mechanics use hand and power tools in their work. They use these for fastening and loosening screws, nuts, and bolts on vehicles and their engines. Auto repair shops have special equipment for heavy lifting. They also use special tools for quickly changing tires. Many shops now have computers. These are used to find out more about what is wrong with a vehicle. Auto repair shops that do bodywork have tools for welding and painting.

Impact Wrenches

These wrenches are used to turn very rusted or worn nuts and bolts. Impact wrenches are very noisy. They twist the nut or bolt in strong, short bursts of about five seconds.

Hand Wrenches

Mechanics use hand wrenches to turn nuts and bolts. The combination wrench has an open and a closed end. These are used for different jobs. Some wrenches are adjustable to fit around different fasteners. Pipe wrenches can turn old or rusty bolts. Socket wrenches come in many shapes and sizes.

Lifts and Hoists

Large auto shops have equipment for raising vehicles off the ground. Jacks lift up part of a vehicle such as a wheel. Some mechanics use a flat creeper cart with wheels. The mechanic lies on this when it is rolled under the vehicle.

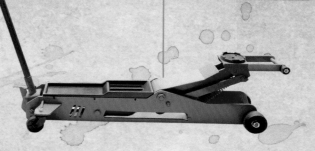

Then

Cars have always needed repairs. The first auto mechanics were experts in high demand. Their work was often poorly paid and dangerous. Mechanics worked on all parts of the vehicle. As new repair technology was invented, mechanics needed to be better trained.

Electronic Diagnostic Equipment

Each vehicle has information from the company that made it. Mechanics check this information using the diagnostic equipment. Most pieces of diagnostic equipment are hand-held devices. Some are on wheels. This means that they can be moved around.

Now

Today, auto mechanics need more training than before. Some specialize on certain parts of a vehicle. They also need to keep up to date as carmakers add new technology. Auto mechanics are now better protected at work. There are also laws to make sure they are fairly paid.

The Mechanic's Role

Motor vehicles are very important to modern society. Many goods are transported by road every day. More than 70 percent of manufactured goods in the U.S. were moved on trucks in 2012. This included food supplies to supermarkets and medical supplies for hospitals. The vehicles used to transport goods need to be maintained and repaired regularly.

Large workstations are needed for the repair and servicing of large vehicles such as trucks.

People also rely on their cars. They drive to work or take their children to school. Mechanics make sure family vehicles are safe for all members of the family to travel in. Auto repair and maintenance work can sometimes be expensive. It can make the car last longer, though. This can save the owner money over a long period of time.

Recycling

Auto repair shops also work to protect the environment. They dispose of hazardous materials carefully. Used tires are sent for recycling. Many parts from old vehicles are recycled to make new parts.

About **95 percent** of vehicles taken off the road in the U.S. each year are recycled.

More than **80 percent** of scrap tires in the U.S. are successfully recycled.

About **95 percent** of auto repair shops recycle vehicle engine oil.

Becoming a Mechanic

To become a mechanic, people have to have the right skills and attitude. Mechanics lift heavy objects. They also deal with dirt, noise, and hazardous materials. They are often at work on holidays, weekends, and into the evenings. Mechanics also need to be in good physical shape. Mechanics make decisions and solve problems. They need a high school diploma and they need to have on-the-job and classroom training.

The number of jobs for mechanics is expected to grow by 17 percent by 2020. Salaries for auto mechanics vary in different areas of the United States. Mechanics earn more money based on their experience in their job. Salaries are also based on the type of job a mechanic does.

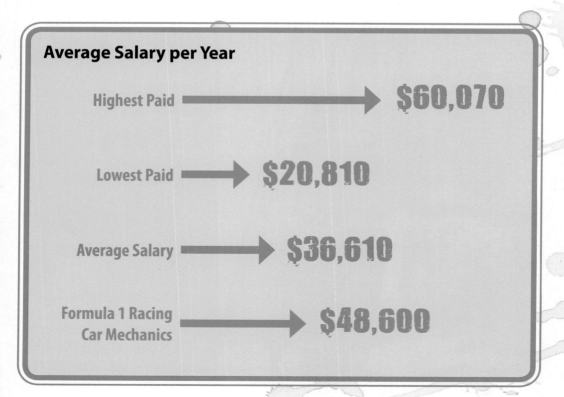

Average Salary per Year

Highest Paid	$60,070
Lowest Paid	$20,810
Average Salary	$36,610
Formula 1 Racing Car Mechanics	$48,600

Many companies require their staff to take tests and get experience on the job before they are hired.

⚠ WARNING

Is This Career For You?

A career as a mechanic is not for everyone. You may enjoy mechanical work and have some or all of the needed skills. However, you may not always be working on vehicles. You might not enjoy reading manuals to learn how to fix problems. Working with computers and electronics can be difficult. It is important to remember that some mechanics are **self-employed**.

✓ ## Training

Mechanics do on-the-job training with experienced workers. They do many kinds of jobs until they start working on vehicle engines. Mechanics also take some classroom courses during their training.

✓ ## Education

Get a high school diploma and take computer courses. High schools have courses in automotive repair or electrical work. Local **trade schools** and colleges also have classes.

✓ ## Application

Contact local auto repair shops about available jobs. City government and private companies who operate vehicle fleets may also have openings. Some positions are advertised on the internet or on job boards.

Career Connections

Plan your career as a mechanic with this activity. Follow the instructions in the steps below to complete the process of becoming a mechanic.

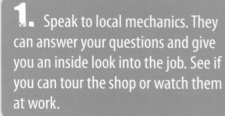

1. Speak to local mechanics. They can answer your questions and give you an inside look into the job. See if you can tour the shop or watch them at work.

2. Visit a job fair or a college career center to find out more information about working as a mechanic.

3. Work on your resumé. A good resumé that shows your strongest skills can go a long way toward attracting the attention of potential employers.

4. Call or write to an auto repair shop. Say that you are interested in a job as a mechanic and ask for advice on how to apply.

1. Decide if you have the personality and attitude for being a mechanic. If you do not mind a dirty and noisy job, can work long hours, and are in good physical shape, this may be the job for you.

2. Consider the skills you will need to have.

3. Contact employers to find out what they are looking for from potential applicants.

4. Apply for the position and arrange an interview. If successful, come to the interview with knowledge of the industry and your skills.

Quiz

1. What percentage of auto mechanics work in shops, dealerships, or in parts stores?

2. What was the average mechanic salary in the U.S. in 2012?

3. What is a creeper cart?

4. How many service technicians and mechanics were there in the United States in 2012?

5. What kind of wrench has an open and a closed end?

6. What does ASE stand for?

7. What is it called when computers are used to find the cause of a vehicle problem?

8. What is a face shield?

9. How many U.S. auto mechanics are estimated to have been exposed to asbestos dust?

10. When do mechanics wear fabric or leather gloves?

Answers: 1. About 70 percent 2. $36,610 3. A flat piece of equipment with wheels that can be rolled under a vehicle 4. 701,100 5. A combination wrench 6. Automotive Service Excellence 7. A diagnostic test 8. A helmet with a clear shield to protect the face and neck 9. About 900,000 10. When welding metal or working with hot exhaust pipes

Key Words

asbestos: a fire resistant material; inhaling its dust is a health hazard

bodywork: the metal outer shell of a vehicle

dealerships: businesses linked to vehicle manufacturers that sell new or used cars

diesel: a heavy fuel used in some engines

ethanol: a colorless liquid that is used in fuel

exhaust: waste gases or air the escapes from an engine

filters: pieces of equipment that strain dirt from the engine of a vehicle

fleets: large groups of vehicles that are under the control of one company

gasoline: a fuel for engines that drive cars and other vehicles

lubricants: oil or grease that is used on engines and other parts of a vehicle

makes: vehicles from a particular company

overtime: time spent working that is in addition to normal working hours

power tools: tools driven by motors

self-employed: working for oneself rather than for an employer

suspension: the part of a vehicle that has springs and shock absorbers connecting the wheels to the body

trade schools: a school that offers training in skilled trades

welding: joining together metal by heating it and pressing it together

Index

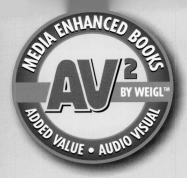

Log on to www.av2books.com

AV² by Weigl brings you media enhanced books that support active learning. Go to www.av2books.com, and enter the special code found on page 2 of this book. You will gain access to enriched and enhanced content that supplements and complements this book. Content includes video, audio, weblinks, quizzes, a slide show, and activities.

AV² Online Navigation

Audio
Listen to sections of the book read aloud

Video
Watch informative video clips.

Embedded Weblinks
Gain additional information for research.

Try This!
Complete activities and hands-on experiments.

Book Pages
AV² pages directly correspond to pages in the book.

Key Words
Study vocabulary, and complete a matching word activity.

Quizzes
Test your knowledge.

Slide Show
View images and captions, and prepare a presentation.

AV² was built to bridge the gap between print and digital. We encourage you to tell us what you like and what you want to see in the future.

Sign up to be an AV² Ambassador at www.av2books.com/ambassador.